KT-162-118

Let's visit a
SHEEP FARM

Sarah Doughty
and
Diana Bentley
Reading Consultant
University of Reading

Photographs by
Chris Fairclough

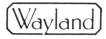
Wayland

Let's Visit a Farm

Beef Farm
Cereal Farm
Dairy Farm
Fish Farm
Fruit Farm
Market Garden
Pig Farm
Poultry Farm
Sheep Farm

First published in 1990 by
Wayland (Publishers) Ltd
61 Western Road, Hove
East Sussex, BN3 1JD, England

© Copyright 1990 Wayland (Publishers) Ltd

British Library Cataloguing in Publication Data
Doughty, Sarah
　　Let's visit a sheep farm.
　　1. English language – Readers
　　I. Title　II. Bentley, Diana
　　III. Doughty, Sarah.
　　Let's visit a farm
　　428.6

　　ISBN 1 85210 748 0

Phototypeset by
Kalligraphics Ltd
Horley, Surrey
Printed and bound by
Casterman S.A., Belgium

Contents

All the words that appear in **bold** are explained in the glossary on page 28.

This is the sheep farm in Wales

Farmhouse

The farm

Indoor pens

Sheep dip

Barn

9

Here is the sheep farmer

Mr Williams is a sheep farmer. He and his family live on a sheep farm in South Wales. They have a flock of Welsh Mountain sheep. For most of the year, the sheep live on the hills surrounding the farm. They grow thick woolly coats to protect them in cold weather. In the winter, some of the **ewes** will be brought inside for lambing.

A lamb is born

The ewes are **mated** with **rams** in October. In February they are ready to give birth to their lambs. Sometimes a ewe has two or three lambs. Mr Williams is helping this ewe give birth to twins.

After a lamb is born, the ewe licks it dry. The lamb soon finds its mother's **udder** and drinks her milk.

The lamb is fed with a bottle

Sometimes a ewe has too many lambs to look after.
This newborn lamb cannot be fed by its mother. So
Mrs Williams is looking after the lamb. She puts it in
a box to keep it warm.

Mrs Williams and her grandson feed the lamb
with milk from a bottle. The lamb is bottle-fed until it
is big enough to be **weaned**.

The sheep are fed extra food

All the sheep are given extra food during the cold winter months. At lambing time the ewes need plenty to eat. The farm worker feeds the ewes with **silage**, and **pellets** of food called concentrate. Concentrate is a mixture of **cereals** with added **minerals**.

The farmer keeps his sheep healthy

Mr Williams gives all his sheep a **vaccine** to stop them catching diseases. He **injects** the vaccine into the sheep's body.

Sheep may catch a disease caused by worms. Worms are tiny creatures that live in a sheep's stomach. The farm worker uses a dosing gun to give the animals a mixture to clear the sheep of worms.

The sheep are sheared

Sheep shearing takes place every summer. The shearers use electric shears to cut the **fleece** from the sheep. Shearers are very skilled at their job. It takes them only one or two minutes to remove a whole fleece. The fleeces are sold and made into wool.

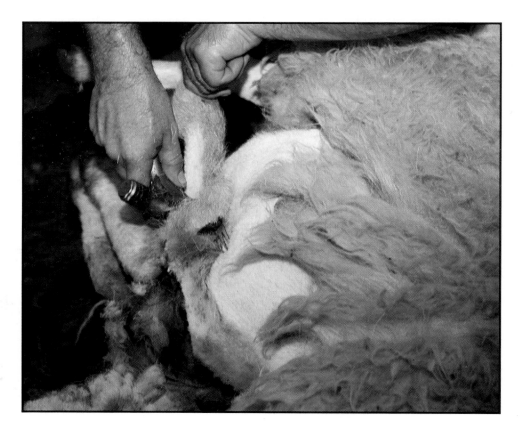

Sheep-dogs are used to round up the sheep

All summer, the sheep live in fields or roam among the hills. When the farmer wants to gather his sheep together he uses working sheep-dogs . The farm worker makes calls and whistles that tell the dogs what to do. The dogs circle the sheep and drive them the right way. These sheep are being rounded up ready to be dipped.

The sheep are dipped to clean their coats

Two weeks after shearing, the farmer baths his sheep in a sheep-dip. This gets rid of any **pests** that are caught in their coats. All the sheep make their way through a bath of **disinfectant**. The farmer has a long pole to push the sheep under for a moment.

These sheep have been dipped. Sheep do not mind dipping as it makes them cool in warm weather.

A stock fair is held at the farm

The Williams are having an autumn stock fair at their farm. At a stock fair, farmers buy and sell sheep. It is also fun for the children as there are competitions and pony rides.

Mr Williams decides which sheep he wants to keep and which ones he wants to sell at the fair. Some of the fatter lambs are sold for meat but others are kept for breeding. The ewes are now mated with rams. They will give birth to lambs next year.

Glossary

Cereals Crops that have a grain that can be eaten.
Disinfectant A chemical substance that kills pests.
Ewes Female sheep.
Fleece A sheep's coat.
Inject To put a medicine into the body using a special, hollow needle.
Mated When a ram and ewe are joined together to produce young.
Minerals All animals and people need to eat tiny amounts of minerals to keep healthy.
Pellets Small, rounded pieces of food.
Pests Unwanted flies, lice or insects in a sheep's coat.
Rams Male sheep.
Silage Cut grass that has been stored and kept moist.
Udder Part of the sheep where milk is made.
Vaccine A medicine that stops a sheep catching diseases.
Weaned When a lamb has begun to eat solid food.

Books to read

Sheep on the Farm by C. Moon (Wayland, 1983)
Sheep Shearing Time by A. Vincent (Young Library, 1988)

Places to visit
Notes for parents and teachers

To find out more about visiting a sheep farm, or any other type of farm in your area, you might like to get in touch with the following organizations:

The Association of Agriculture (Farm Visits Service), Victoria Chambers, 16–20 Strutton Ground, London SW1P 2HP.
They have produced a useful booklet called *Farms to Visit in Britain* which gives details of farms that are open to the public, many with special facilities for schools.

The National Union of Farmers, Agriculture House, 25–31 Knightsbridge, London SW1X 7NJ.
Local branches organize visits to farms. Their addresses can be obtained from your library.

County Colleges of Agriculture
These exist in most counties. Many have an established Schools Liaison or Environmental Studies Unit. Contact the Association of Agriculture if you have difficulty in locating your local College of Agriculture.

Acknowledgement

The publishers would like to thank the farmer and his family for their help and co-operation in the making of this book.

Index